I0505774

Free Gift

I wanted to thank you for getting this book and as a Free Gift I would like to share with you a 7-point checklist to help you optimize your LinkedIn profile for more sales connections and opportunities.

Get Your Free Profile Optimization Checklist

Just visit

http://linkedonautopilot.com/profilechecklist2/

I hope you love it.

Thanks again for supporting my work!

Contents

Introduction

This book contains proven steps and strategies on how to generate more marketing leads using the world's largest professional social network, LinkedIn. With this book, you will see that spending just least ten minutes a day will give you the opportunity to broaden your professional networking prospects on LinkedIn. This Book also gives you practical insights into how you turn your connections on one of the world's fastest growing online networking platforms into what can generate quality leads with clients that matter. It can also help you build loyalty to your services or products - that may also include you as a potential recruit for an employer if that's what you are seeking.

Thanks for getting this book. I hope you enjoy it!

Chapter 1: What is LinkedIn?

Social networking is not the bleeding edge technology it was when first introduced almost a decade ago. But how far you go and what benefits you stand to gain from your wide or narrow social networking connections remains one of the most tantalizingly elusive questions today. In many people's minds, social networking usually means Facebook and Twitter. However, going social on the Internet and building networks would not be beneficial if we couldn't turn the connections we establish into something meaningful from which we can reap short and long term benefits. That was the premise behind the founding of LinkedIn by Reid Hoffman. His desire was to find a way for people around the world to interact by posting updates, sharing pictures, and creating something that would bring users profitable returns in either the short or long run.

LinkedIn is the world's largest online professional social networking site. Since it's founding in 2002, LinkedIn has not just helped connect people but it has been one of the most influential recruitment platforms where employers look for potential hires. On LinkedIn, there is a balance between passive and active sharing. It is not just about posting and sharing pictures for fun. It's about sharing the knowledge, experiences and marketing through your profile so that it stands out conspicuously to clients who are out there looking for your expertise or those employers looking for your skills.

LinkedIn has helped many find their dream jobs in a matter of weeks or even just a few days. If you are looking for an opportunity, chances are overwhelming that potential employers are looking on LinkedIn for the skills they need for their teams. If you don't have a profile on the world's largest professional online network, you are missing out on getting found among potential candidates. But how can you differentiate yourself from the many other candidates? We'll look at that in a moment but for now the question that many people would probably be asking is what makes LinkedIn so different from Facebook or Twitter or even Tumblr?

Simply put, Facebook has grown over the years into one of the world's most active marketing platforms where companies can reach out to millions of prospective clients within the shortest time possible. LinkedIn has established itself as a platform where the primary form of networking is largely surrounding professional engagement.

Also, the popularity of LinkedIn has been primarily established as a platform for marketing oneself for professional engagements such as a job hunt. Over the last few years, it has also made it an ideal platform where marketers can build great company profiles and sell to targeted clients. Based on research, it is quickly apparent that people focus on their work-related experiences on LinkedIn rather than the more entertainment-based sharing that occurs on Facebook. With Facebook friends search and connect with strangers based on what interests they share and the content that they share. But that's not to say there is no sharing on LinkedIn, but rather the difference is in the way content is shared and the overall end goal for members. We will talk about that a bit more in a coming chapter but for now just remember that LinkedIn has become the 'virtual Rolodex' for people seeking opportunities on a professional level.

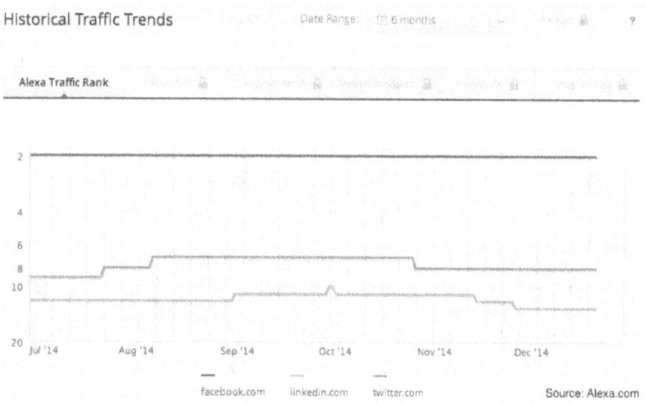

Activity 1:

Think about five possible ways through which LinkedIn can practically and productively be used to achieve professional goals such as marketing and image projection to employers.

Chapter 2: LinkedIn Etiquette

Etiquette is a necessary skill in any human encounter, particularly if you are in a professional setting like an office. It is especially crucial if you interact with people online and aim to build on your reputation. On social networks such as Facebook and Twitter, people have more often than not breached prescribed codes of conduct in many ways perhaps without even realizing it. With the speed at which information travels, bad etiquette can rapidly disseminate and do damage to your reputation. What some people don't understand is that it is more important than ever to portray a professional image on LinkedIn that inspires confidence and builds your credibility.

Essentially, LinkedIn is not a place that users expect to waste significant time sharing material that doesn't somehow create value for other users. Profile views on LinkedIn have the potential to earn you the ideal connections that can grow your network effectively. Treat your profile and what you share on the platform with respect. By displaying a profile you're proud to share, you are increasing the chances of generating great inbound connections. But first things first, let's take a sneak preview into what codes of conduct you ought to abide by on LinkedIn.

Avoid The Numbers Game

As opposed to social networking media like Facebook and Twitter where many aim at building fame or popularity based on their number of connections or followings, in LinkedIn, a "less is more" approach can help you generate more leads. Remember, it is better to be connected to a few companies that define your professional interests and target prospects than having many connections and little or no engagement because of a poorly constructed profile.

Give timely response to connection requests

LinkedIn is all about professional connections and creating leads that allow you to target your most valuable prospects (either employers or clients). It is always important that you check in regularly to see if you have connection requests in your notification box. Try to be responsive to the requests or better yet, review your LinkedIn "To Do" items for a few minutes each morning as part of your routine. Making this a part of your day establishes it as a critical component of your targeting and inbound attraction strategy.

Your profile picture says a lot so make it professional

Like it or not, most of us are visual people and we respond to photos. Having a photo is an invaluable contribution to profile proficiency. Your picture is something that a potential employer or client can use to evaluate your professional image and at the very least it helps them see if you understand LinkedIn etiquette. Profile pictures are essential to social networking. On Facebook or Twitter, you can put up any picture without potential repercussions. Putting up a photo that portrays you in a non-professional light on LinkedIn could cost you a dream job or even invaluable marketing prospects.

Even if you land your dream gig, stay active

Employers are hard lot to understand sometimes. They value employees on many different levels. Say you are looking for a job in a marketing and sales company and, you happen to land one via LinkedIn. Having accomplished your goal, you go dormant on LinkedIn.

But what many LinkedIn users don't realize is that the platform is essential in how you position you in the market and, potentially prospective employers still weigh your activity as one of their evaluation criteria. Basically they are looking for reputation and credibility in your given area of expertise. This is often difficult for people to come to grips with but just as brands and companies reach out to engage with their potential customers, you should also be regularly engaging with your target prospects. If you neglect the opportunity to engage, you effectively will have lost some value in the eyes of a potential client or employer and the ability for them to get a better idea of what value you can offer. Staying active gives you a way to be open to a better opportunity, which you might miss by failing to engage on the platform. New connections matter and regular engagement with your network is even more valuable over the long-term.

Do not rush building connections and pitching leads to prospects

Sometimes the worst thing you can do that could cost you an opportunity is to rush into finalizing a relationship that is just in the early stages. On LinkedIn where you are largely searching for new prospects, this could be even more detrimental. People move from strangers to acquaintances and then to friends. Whenever you make new connections on LinkedIn, creating a rapport that builds trust is all that you need to win loyalty of prospects and lasting good impression on a potential employer. Don't rush too quickly to try and close: share content of value to your target and build credibility over time.

Make your connection and recommendation requests speak on your behalf

The best way you can build relationships is speak out in the most professional, passionate and friendly way you can. LinkedIn has a feature that allows you to personalize the message that briefly explains why you need the other person to connect with you. The reason why this is valuable (and increases your response rate for connections) is that instead of sending the default connection request with the standard message it shows that you have gone the extra mile to get to know a bit about your prospective connection. This way, you will create a first impression that will remain a lasting impression in their mind. It allows you to stand out from others that are just sending connection requests to increase their numbers and shows you as a professional networker that is working to achieve mutual benefit for both parties.

Build and grow relationships

In real world, collaboration thrives based on how often you keep in touch with other group members to share tasks and discuss project deliverables. The same applies for LinkedIn. There are many ways to grow your network and make strong bonds with your connections. LinkedIn has group forums where you can actively engage in discussions. You can also build engagement by posting and sharing what interests your connections. This way your network will expand and it will also keep you top of mind with your network, improving your chances of landing your most desired opportunities.

Stay professional if at all possible. Do not ask your LinkedIn connects to follow you on Facebook

One of the most common errors new users make is to ask their connections to follow them on social sites like Facebook where the level of professional engagement is arguably not as sophisticated as LinkedIn. You risk losing your most valuable prospects if you do this as the general level of conversations and sharing may not be what's needed to build that all-important credibility and trust.

From its earliest days, LinkedIn has been and has remained a professional social networking site where marketers pitch to clients, managers look for potential employees and employees seek connections that could land them their dream job. As I mentioned previously this is not necessarily the case with other social sites like Facebook where sharing of pictures or posts is not primarily to build professional engagement. So, keep the jokes to a minimum unless you really know your network's preferences for this type of content.

You also want to avoid posting content too frequently in any given period. Over posting can give your connections the sense that you are using LinkedIn as just another way to "broadcast" so limit your posts and shares to a maximum of two daily.

Adjust your notifications so that your network is visible to your connections

For most users there is an understanding of reciprocity, which underlies what makes LinkedIn an effective social network. As it is such an effective as a way to breed professional relationships and achieve long-term engagement with clients, it is a great way to add value to your relationships with the power of your network. As you share content, professional experiences and marketing ideas, your network benefits. And the larger your network so to speak, the larger the benefit. So let you connect see your connections as much as they let you see theirs.

Activity 2:

Sharing content successfully on LinkedIn requires a long-term view of your relationships and what they might find valuable. As you browse the web today think of 5 things that you can share with your network that benefits them (not just you).

Chapter 3: What your profile says about you and how to stand out to your prospects

A picture is always said to be a thousand words and when it comes to LinkedIn, how you make you profile stand out is could be worth a thousand connections. There are many LinkedIn users who share in the same profession as you do. This means, they too are looking for same connections as you are. However, if you review their network, you might see some differences in the how they've tailored their experience, what they currently do, as well as their recommendations, skills and expertise. Compare this with how your profile displays and fine-tune yours wherever necessary. Take a look at this quick video (http://goo.gl/rMJ4vF) at how you can do this using Google Chrome.

With over 300 million users, getting your seen profile in LinkedIn requires you to stand out to your targets. Here are a few things to consider:

A profile picture is worth a thousand words

Profile pictures in social media platforms really do speak volumes and it's quite unfortunate that many people often take this for granted. First according to the LinkedIn blog those profiles with a picture get more than eleven times he number of views as those profiles without a picture. Many people who have used LinkedIn to carry out successful marketing campaigns attribute it partly to a professional profile picture. And if you don't have a profile picture now it's not too late. Adding a one can make a marked difference in the number of profile views your get.

Compare this to two websites, one packed with textual content, and the other packed with an infusion of images and text that captivates the reader. It's pretty easy to see that the latter is more approachable to your potential clients.

A clear headline that is image focused

Let's take a look at a simple but powerful example. Think about what newspapers without headlines would look like. Chances are they would draw a fraction of the readership because the headlines reinforce the big story in each article, getting the viewers to want to read further. In LinkedIn, your profile description (or your headline) adds immense value to your profile image and therefore allows you to attract better-targeted prospects. The use of keywords that relate to your profession (and reinforce what your targets are looking for) would add additional ways for the LinkedIn search algorithm to find and surface your profile in a search.

Let's illustrate this. Perhaps you are a journalist and you're trying to pitch yourself on LinkedIn.

Your main target would likely be news agencies and media organizations that are looking for professional journalists. Thinking about what your potential target would be looking for on LinkedIn would suggest including some specific keywords in your profile description based on your experience, skills, and goals. But just a word of caution: don't go too far in "keyword-stuffing." LinkedIn's search algorithm does penalize profiles that go overboard in layering on the keywords. In the case of the journalist, if an employer is looking for specific skills, they might come up first among their search results depending on how well crafted their profile description was for the right keywords.

Your summary should make you stand out to prospects and stick in their minds

Standing out in one thing doesn't necessarily mean screaming the same thing over and over. But keeping top of mind provides long-term value to sales and marketing. Words themselves can help prospects remember the value you deliver as well as having a great picture that sticks in the mind.

On LinkedIn, as long as you are hunting for a job, your summary ought to display you as the best solution to your target's problems. Ensure you project yourself through a carefully and professionally crafted summary that shows that you know what your potential clients are feeling. This will go beyond reinforcing your picture. In this example below a lawyer shows he truly understands some of the pains his clients have gone through and he grabs their attention so that they read more.

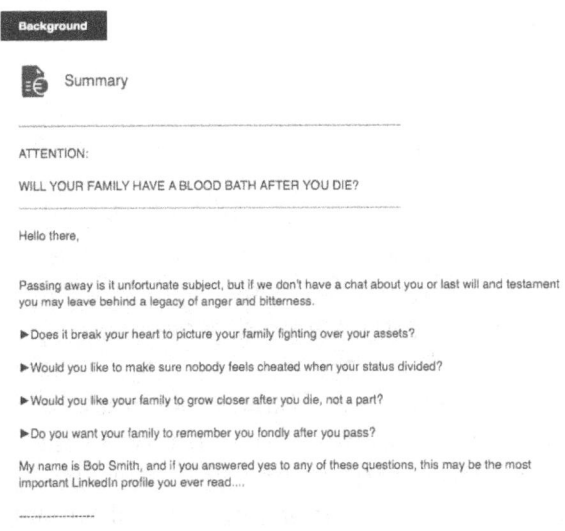

Make your summary stand out so that it resonates with your prospects

How you display your achievements matters: Give your experiences, skills and knowledge value at a first glance

Potential clients or employers have no time to wade through volumes of text. All they need is a short, precise and clear display of your achievements and how you can help them achieve their goals. Show that you understand the value of their time by letting them understand the key things about you at a first glance. You can make this possible by always ensuring your experiences comes first then followed by a professionally crafted description of experiences and skills.

Some people do this with a media in which they display their experiences and skills as video portfolio. Other use video to pitch themselves to prospects using a short clip that take less than three minutes where they describe themselves, experiences, knowledge, skills and how they can help. This can definitely be an effective way to communicate but make sure it is something that is professionally done. Think about what you want to communicate, write a draft and practice it in front of the mirror. When you are ready to do the actual video, consider what it would look like to a prospect so you can plan ahead to put your best foot forward.

Status updates and posts improve your visibility

There are thousands of LinkedIn profiles that lie idle and wasted. The reason likely is that the owners of such profiles rushed to put something on the platform without asking themselves why they even needed an account in the first place. This is not unique to LinkedIn. In fact on Twitter research estimated that almost half (428 Million of the 974 Million registered users) have never posted anything on the network. With LinkedIn you have to be able to answer the question "what do I want to accomplish by putting my information on the platform?"

If you decide to say ten minutes a day on LinkedIn, you will get better results if you understand your overall goal so that you can focus your efforts. And there are a variety of things you can do on the site that will help you get to where you want to go. But a great profile is only part of the picture. You could have the best profile on the entire site but what if you hardly update anything or do any posting?

Updating and posting on a regular basis is part of separates ordinary users from the extraordinary. This means, even spending ten minutes a day on this platform can generate a noticeable ROI for your business and your image. Sharing content such as posting articles in your updates ensures that your prospects notice you and helps you stand out in your field. It takes a little bit of effort to get noticed on an active site like LinkedIn but in the end it is not that hard to stand out and doesn't require a ton of time.

Group participation broadens your impact

LinkedIn, just like Facebook, has groups and forums that help you connect, share and discuss. Groups are opportunities for sharing ideas and, you should always ways to take advantage of this powerful channel to connect and engage.

But as mentioned earlier the way you engage and your sensitivity to the conversations with potential prospects makes the difference. As you participate in groups, you will likely come across other group members that fit your target prospect criteria. This is a great opportunity to connect with the group connection feature. You can see more about how to go about this here. Simply note his or her name so that you can send a professionally crafted and personalized connection request. This will enable you to get to know each other outside the group as a connection and build a longer-term relationship.

Put your current role in the best light- never forget to ask for recommendations

Many people who are looking for a new position fear that showing their current employment information might cost them their dream job. Worse still, they fear that by there could be negative repercussions in their current position if a potential employer browsed their profile.

However, fears of this are largely overblown. In fact, you can change your settings to turn off broadcasts of your network activity so others can't see that you have updated your experience or profile, in general.

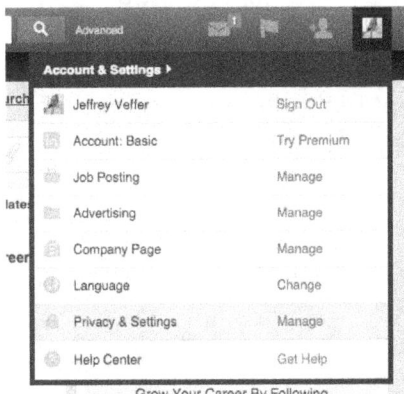

From the home page hover over your photo in the top right and select Privacy and Settings.

From Profile select "Turn off your activity broadcasts"

Activity 3:

There are many ways you can make your profile identifiable by potential connections on LinkedIn. Think about at least five ways that will make your profile speak on your behalf. Infuse them into your current LinkedIn account and see if your profile views increase.

Chapter 4: Opportunities: Generating opportunities using your weak ties and your broader network

In archery, hitting the target is the name of the game. Simply defined players win based on how precise they are when it comes to hitting the right places. On LinkedIn finding great opportunities works on the same principle. The difference on LinkedIn is that you reach the right prospects not just with a great profile but also how you maximize on your weak ties within the broader network of the LinkedIn community.

Opportunities are out there, but the bottom line is that they will not necessarily just drop into your lap. It's up to you to go out there and look for them. Remember, there is competition and how well you project yourself really matters. In the professional world, the established practice that gets people great opportunities is networking. The difference online is that the reach and speed of interaction are different than in face-to-face networking.

The basic role of networking is uncovering an opportunity for value exchange arising out of the interaction. But there is also a hidden benefit that might not be apparent at first glance. It pays off if, with every connection, you craft a relationship that will help you even if the initial opportunity to that person is not immediately there.

In this chapter, we take a look at why you need to take a determined approach to networking. But first let's zero in on the meaning of weak ties.

Demystifying weak ties in networking

Social fabric is what knits our relationships with friends and acquaintances in the real world. With the advent of online social media networking we now have diminished boundaries because we can actually connect with someone who is thousands of miles away from us even if we have never met them in the physical world. This is one aspect that makes networking interesting but it provides a paradox. It is so easy to connect to someone we've never met in person that sometimes we don't truly know the people we are connected to and can't recall ever connecting with them.

In a networking relationship, codes of communication can either be explicit or implicit. When we connect, share and get in touch with close friends online, the modes of communication are often implicit and part of the social norms that we inherently understand as we use sites like LinkedIn. In research published in the early 1970's Mark Granovetter proposed that we need both strong ties (close friends) as well as weak ties (acquaintances) to form social bonds. In talking to subjects who had recently changed, jobs he found that the most valuable information about the prospective job had come from the job seeker's weak ties. One of the hypotheses about the underlying reason is that if information about the prospective job were relatively rare, the job-seekers strong ties (close friends) would not have any more information than the job seeker. This assumes that the strong ties share information equally among themselves. It would take a weak tie to have access to information outside of this close group of friends to provide new input to the job seeker.

Through weak ties, you can build bridges that help you connect with different groups in social media. Your weak ties will them help you cultivate relationships or connections with friends of friends. Before you know it, your network is creating opportunities on LinkedIn.

With this knowledge on how weak ties play an instrumental role when it comes to networking, your chances of finding opportunities or opportunities finding you are multiplied many times. In fact, it is your weak ties that broaden your networking on LinkedIn and consequently the opportunity to reach out to people you never knew existed. You can then begin to build relationships that could generate leads and other opportunities.

Cultivate opportunities out of your broader network

From the seemingly infinite world of online networking, you can cultivate opportunities and skills that will help you achieve more in the real world. As you interact with people in your LinkedIn network (both with those you know at a personal level and those who you define as your weak ties,) you may at some point pick up a marvelous idea from a LinkedIn group discussion. Say it was 'how to cultivate a good working relationship through imagery.' You might try putting in place the idea at your workplace or in a conference. What results could just help you stand out especially if this idea is not well implemented in your area of expertise. As word gets out you, will find that you could become better known in your field, which can attract even more opportunities.

Essentially, LinkedIn is a place where you nurture your network and engage with friends and your weak ties. You can set yourself up for success either in your hunt for opportunities or at your workplace. Learn from what your broader network and share with them even better ideas. This discussion helps you cultivate a great story about you, which helps you build authority and credibility in your network.

Activity 4:

After your next face-to-face networking event, connect with those you met on LinkedIn. Follow up to see if there are things that you have in common that might help each of you in your respective roles.

Chapter 5: Targeting -Identify your ideal client and their interests

Spending ten minutes a day on LinkedIn can yield productive sales and marketing leads if you carefully pick your target. Depending on what idea or product you want to sell or even what career you want, your prospects must ideally be interested in you based on their assessment of your skills and experience.

Having spent some time on your profile, let's take a look at how you can get even more views through a careful selection of ideal clients so you can reach the right target niche.

Draft a list of companies you want to do business with

Prospecting on LinkedIn is a challenging task because there are millions of companies and individuals who could potentially be interested in your product. On LinkedIn, there is a search box that enables you to look for and identify companies of interest and decide if they are the right ones to target.

However, what should come first is your assessment of your professional background (including your skills and service offering) and how you would want to build a relationship with that company.

To illustrate this assume you are running a furniture rental business, and you want to sign a contract with an event management company. What makes your furniture rental business and an events company a good fit for a potential relationship is the fact there are complimentary needs. Your business requires an event management company as a channel to reach more clients that are holding events. Prospecting, for this reason, becomes easier because you know the most likely relationships to build that would increase your business. Now we come to the next issue about targeting your ideal clients or company.

Establish common ground

Common ground is what makes businesses work together. Staying with the example of your furniture rental business and the event management company, the common ground is that the customers very often need furniture during events. In the majority of cases, event management companies do not always provide furniture rental as part of their in-house services because they are more concerned about managing the entire event and can outsource this service. This is where your furniture rental business comes in. Once you have made arrangements to work together and established a quality relationship, prospecting becomes easier.

How well are you connected?

In trying to connect with potential partners to market your products and services, it is pivotal that you review how well you are connected. This is where weak ties and broader connections come into play. As mentioned previously weak ties can become an essential part of your strategy to get exposed to more business opportunities that are outside of your close network of friends and associates. As another example, a company that provides cleaning services requires more connections with business that contract cleaning services like banks and airports. If your company provides cleaning services, does you have connections that could put you in touch with decision makers at these potential partners? It is always easier to reach out to a company through an individual who works there than through the "official representative" of company itself because the official channel might not know your skills and experience as well as the channels to get a decision made.

It is a balancing act. You want to provide just enough information to move your request along the decision path, but not overwhelm your 'weak tie' connection with too much material that turns them off helping you. You need to be a good judge of the amount of time they are spending assisting you. Make it as easy as possible for them. Don't attached massive files to emails. Make your message very straightforward so they don't have to re-write or interpret anything that you want to say. In fact, if you can write the email so they can just forward it on all the better.

Group discussions are great forums for connecting with ideal clients

LinkedIn is a powerful platform with many ways to create great business opportunities. With the numerous ways to connect and build relationships, it's no surprise that many people do not realize the power of using LinkedIn groups in connecting and partnering. Group membership is a great tool for prospecting. As long as you are a group member you can connect with other group members that are part of your target market for your business or service offering. It is a great place to target your most attractive clients.

First, prospecting requires you to establish common goals and interests with individuals within your group and companies. You will have a better chance to find the right opportunities when you need them.

Sharing an event can attract the right prospects

Sharing an event you are hosting (or participating in) is an often-overlooked method to attract prospects, but it can pay off powerfully. It gives you the opportunity to build anticipation and a great opportunities to create value for attendees, especially if you have done your research on what your prospects would like to find out about and who they would like to network with.

But like anything on the platform, a certain degree of professionalism should underpin your efforts. The event doesn't have to be a huge tradeshow by any means, but even if it's a meet up, you should consider how it would look to potential attendees. For example, a short video clip that shows your business and allows you to put a 'face' to the event can help your event to break through the clutter of information facing your prospects.

When you share information about an event on LinkedIn (for instance a sales and marketing seminar), the first impression to your connections is that you are a sales and marketing executive. Marketing the event on LinkedIn through posts and on various forums as well as sending invitations to your connections will amplify the awareness.

Because you are leading with value by creating an event that can benefit attendees in a variety of ways (content sharing, potential relationships) you are reinforcing your image as someone who knows the industry and can bring the right people together – a very valuable combination.

A website helps you target ideal clients

One thing to keep in mind is that even though LinkedIn is a tremendously powerful platform it is still something that you don't totally control. For example, if next week LinkedIn Corporation decided to change some of the key features of the platform, you would have no direct recourse to change their decision. You might, however, be able to gather some support through your network and groups, but it is important to keep in mind that a channel you control wholly is an essential part of your online presence.

You may have your own a website at the moment and your profile is a great place to include a link to it. But instead of the default name "My Website," a little bit of creativity will enable you to connect to target clients by understanding what they want to accomplish. For instance, if you are a sales executive, you can replace the name "My Website" with something that you specialize in - say something like "Sales leads that work magic." This helps you to again communicate more effectively with your prospects by speaking in their language.

Activity 5: How else can you ensure that your target prospects find you instead of you going out of you way to look for them as discussed in this chapter?

Chapter 6: What to post/share

LinkedIn shares many aspects of other social media platforms with the notable exception that it is more professional in terms of what you should post and share within your network, to groups and on your profile. As we earlier noted with LinkedIn etiquette, the same should guide you on what to post and share with your connection so that what you do adds value to your network. People tend to post and share what helps them grow professionally and expand their network of professionals leading to new and better opportunities. In this chapter, we take a look at what you ought to share and post on LinkedIn.

Company Insights

Most LinkedIn users create profiles on the site to grow their professional network by connecting with people who pursue similar interests. They also may be interested in getting updates on company profiles that assist with their job-hunting efforts. According to LinkedIn posts that get more engagement are those that revolve around giving users company insights. If you're a sales executive, posting insights of how companies are handling marketing and sales would be an ideal thing to do. You may also generate some discussion about your post that would help you engage your connections and improve your exposure through enhanced profile views.

Company news

Companies are always looking for outstanding recruits and one of the ways that they can attract suitable talent is through company news. The same data from LinkedIn shows that company news runs a close second after company insights as the most read posts on the site. One of the ways to do this is to comb the internet and source news that relates to companies that have an impact on your profession.

Posts on new services and products

Every day, a new product hits the market. You yourself may or may not need it but what makes a product sell is how well its value proposition is crafted. Again going back to an earlier example if you are a sales executive, capturing the attention of your LinkedIn connections is easier with posts that review products and services related to your profession. Remember, on a social website, a post is never complete until it is shared. However, be professional when posting anything and limit them to a maximum of two posts per day.

Posts on your expertise

One of the best ways to market yourself and perhaps your products on LinkedIn is to post and share items on your skills and expertise. Employers will always be looking for someone who is experienced and up to date will the latest trends in the market. It is, therefore, important that whenever you login to post something, do it with utmost profession. Remembering to regularly update your experience and achievement sections can really attract new interest from your network. To further reinforce this, LinkedIn sends out weekly email notifications to your network telling them about updates to your profile. Keep yourself top of mind to take advantage of this opportunity!

Status update and blog posts

Knowing what to post and when to post it on LinkedIn is important. Of the most posted items on LinkedIn are status updates followed closely by blogs posts. These come after company news, company insights and product reviews. The only difference between a status update and blog posts is that the former tends to be shorter, usually geared to sharing with the latter generally is a bit more in depth and can relate to marketing your products or services. Because studies by social media experts have shown that people are mostly active on LinkedIn in the morning and afternoon, it is the best time to update a status and share your relevant posts around noon or early evening, Monday to Friday. This is because you are catching your network when they have a few minutes around lunch or near the end of the day when they are re-focusing away from their daily tasks.

Activity 6: While it could be worth it posting and sharing within your connections, sometimes it works even better to win more prospects outside your LinkedIn network. How can a video clip help you to engage prospects? Create a clip of say three minutes explaining a bit more about you and your offering and see if it will improve your LinkedIn connections or profile views.

Chapter 7: Getting your posts seen by the right prospects and connecting with the right people

Countless times, LinkedIn has been mentioned as the world's leading professional networking site. And it's also the world's largest site targeted at helping professionals with job hunting and marketing. Most people have created profiles on LinkedIn to network with companies, sell products, and market services but even then, there is more to all of these than just creating a post and sharing it blindly. Before your post and share anything, ask yourself a question: "Are my posts getting seen by my target prospects?" If the answer to this is "No" or "I'm not sure" here's how to plan your campaign with more precision.

You could have the most engaging ideas and relevant expertise, but even that is never a guarantee that someone will eventually come across your content or send you a personal message inviting you to connect.

Whenever you post and share anything on LinkedIn you should do a little background work to give it the best chance to land in the right place and at the right time. Posts that completely miss the mark in terms of content would not interest people who largely are looking to solve a problem or find out more about a certain topic. This means you must be good at prospecting and profiling to find the right group that resonates with what you will be posting. There are a number of ways you can do this.

Group posts and shares

LinkedIn groups provide a powerful tool for prospecting that gives many possibilities for smart marketers. Groups are great forums for sharing relevant content. The keyword is relevant. Most group owners make sure that what gets shared makes it worthwhile for members to view, engage and discuss. So always think about the 'long game' and ensure that you are not sharing blindly but are adding value.

Through groups, you can easily identify people with whom you share similar interests and send them personalized connection requests. But again, try to make your connection request helpful and relevant. There have been cases of users having their accounts restricted because the tried to connect with too many group members in a confined amount of time.

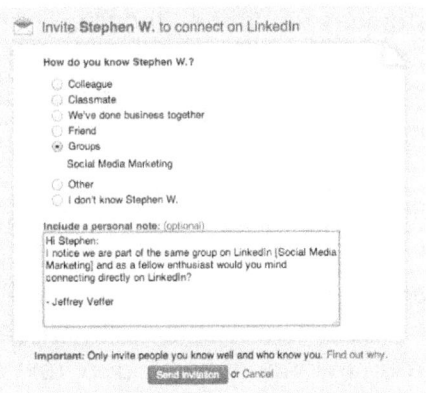

Make your connections count-customize your note.

Know people in your network and prospect based on interests

Once you connect you should note key profile attributes that overlap amongst your connections. Are they in a sales-focused role? Perhaps they have a technical background. All these attributes can help you to continually refine what you are sharing to generate more interest and opportunities.

As just mentioned, blanket sharing of content can land you in "LinkedIn Jail." This is because not everyone is interested in everything you post and share with them on LinkedIn. Within your network, there could be people who are interested in events that target marketers and there could also be people who are looking for job opportunities within healthcare. Therefore, as you post, customize whom you are prospecting at so that you share relevant posts within a relevant niche.

Activity 7:

Posting is never enough until you share. Try out different modes of posting on LinkedIn and see which strategy works better: video, text or a combination of both (multimedia). LinkedIn makes it easy – just put a link or multimedia into the share box on your homepage. Try it!

Chapter 8: LinkedIn on the go: mobile opportunities

Mobile and particularly with mobile marketing is changing the way people seek and find opportunities. With an estimated 6.8 billion subscribers worldwide, (almost the world's population!) mobile marketing and advertising has a scope wider than estimated when the mobile phone was created for voice communication over 2 decades ago. Though in actuality mobile marketing is an extension of online marketing, it is generating more traction than marketers projected.

Social Media sites have been early leaders in tapping into the great potential of mobile marketing by integrating online marketing with mobile friendly messaging. LinkedIn is among the top investors in mobile technology, preferring to refer to it not the "Mobile First" strategy (they say that was 2013) but as **"Platform First."**

While it could be categorized under new and emerging media and technology, mobile marketing is today one of the widely used means of finding jobs or new partnerships. When you signed up for a LinkedIn profile, there was a place where you likely entered your mobile phone number. There is another option that asks you to subscribe to or turn on mobile alerts so that whenever there is a notification or message in your LinkedIn inbox, it comes direct to your phone as a text message.

For those who own smart phones, the second wave of LinkedIn mobile will add to their mobile applications. For those who aren't familiar with 'apps' these are a program or application you can download from the Apple App Store or Google Play Store, install it and experience another level of networking on the go with LinkedIn. You receive LinkedIn alerts on your phone anytime they hit your inbox and all you have to do is open the app and respond.

LinkedIn has 'unbundled' several key features of their original app into many other apps that are focused on certain areas. LinkedIn Connected is one example that gives you relevant updates right on the home screen of the app so you can get up-to-date information on your connections and reach out to them to continue to strengthen your relationship. The app also features what LinkedIn calls 'anticipatory computing', which syncs your contacts and calendars to give you reminders prior to your meetings. These reminders include details of other meeting attendees such as any shared connections and interests so that you have a way to quickly build relationships in the meeting and afterward.

There is also the LinkedIn Pulse app that allows you to create custom feeds of information that you can scan and share to your network with just a few clicks. It is well designed and also allows you to share content to not only your LinkedIn account, but also Facebook and Twitter as well.

To this end, it is important to note that consistently updating and improving your LinkedIn profile and sharing content should be part of your daily tasks that help build your relationships. Every day, try to think about designating ten minutes to getting on LinkedIn to share content, reach out to new connections to bolster your efforts to build your inbound funnel of opportunities.

Chapter 9- Consistency and Automation

The nature of social platforms like LinkedIn is that not only do they reward the sharing of great content, but in order to stay top of mind with your prospects or potential employers, you need to maintain a certain level of frequency. That doesn't mean spamming groups or becoming obtrusive but think of each status update or share as adding to a savings account. A small (but valuable) contribution now can pay off big dividends in the future.

Better yet as the old saying goes, make the process systematic at the source so you don't have to think about it and waste precious decision time when you could be hard-pressed to come up with something relevant.

There are many tools out there that can help in making the sharing process less daunting. One of the most popular is Buffer. On their site, they say that, "*Buffer is the best way to drive traffic, increase fan engagement and save time on social media."* In using it, there are several ways that it helps save time. It allows you to schedule your updates throughout the day and week, so you can spend time all at once (perhaps at the beginning of the week) to queue up a bunch of content and then have it be posted automatically when you want throughout the week.

It also suggests content for you to share based on your profile that may be of interest to your prospects and connections. They also have an extension that you can put into your browser that allows you to share great content that you see as you are browsing throughout your day.

Zapier is an automation tool that many people find useful for tasks such as automatically updating a spreadsheet if someone signs up to their email list. In this case, you can see in this video (https://www.youtube.com/watch?v=yYwXszHLCV8), how Zapier can automatically add your new connections to your CRM program freeing you from having to do this on your own. There are also ways to streamline some of your social media tasks as well. Check out the site and see the creative ways people are using the platform to help them become more efficient.

Conclusion

Thank you again for downloading this book! You've taken the first step towards using LinkedIn to build your network and strengthen your business relationships.

The next step is taking action! This doesn't have to take hours and hours, but can consist of just taking 10 minutes each day to optimize your profile, share relevant content or reach out to other users who you'd like to connect with. And think of the time you spend as an investment: a little bit now could pay off big time later with a new opportunity!

Finally if you enjoyed this book, would you mind taking two minutes to leave an honest review? Reviews are very important to writers like me and it would mean a huge amount if you could do that. I look forward to reading it!

Thank you!

Free Resources:

I didn't set out to write this book for fame or fortune. I wrote it because I really felt passionate about sharing over a decade's experience on LinkedIn so that it could help other people build their network and find great opportunities to enrich their lives.

Statistics show that most people don't get beyond the first chapter of a book. Well, congratulations! You've reached the end and now it's time to put this knowledge to work.

Here are several ways that you can use the information in this book.

Check out a few of the free videos I have put together that go a bit deeper into areas that I couldn't cover in the book. (Type them in carefully, they are case sensitive)

Use Advanced Search to Target The Right Prospects For Your Sales Campaigns-
http://goo.gl/cS7Pkj

Generate more connections and insight about your target prospects by understanding the profile view data -
http://goo.gl/cS7Pkj

Get more referrals from LinkedIn for your sales efforts by leveraging your network- http://goo.gl/og4BLe

Using the find function for insight on prospects or competitors - http://goo.gl/rMJ4vF

Free Gift

I wanted to thank you for getting this book and as a Free Gift I would like to share with you a 7-point checklist to help you optimize your LinkedIn profile for more sales connections and opportunities.

Just visit

http://linkedonautopilot.com/profilechecklist2/

I hope you love it.

Thanks again for supporting my work!